My Miracle Man

My Miracle Man

The Deaths and Life of a
Seven-Organ Transplant Recipient

By Carrie Meehan

FIRST PAPERBACK EDITION PUBLISHED 2024

Design and layout by Dean Graves

Photograph on front cover, pages 2, 19, 42, 60, and 84 by Sam Tremayne

ISBN 978-0-578-27735-6

10 9 8 7 6 5 4 3 2 1

Dedications

TODD: TO MY ANONYMOUS DONOR

Thank you for the gift of life. Not a day goes by that
I don't think of you and am grateful for you.

TO DR. RODRIGO VIANNA

For leading with your heart, for your passionate
advocacy and skill, for knowing that miracles are real,
and for never giving up on Todd.

TO OUR FRIEND KYLE BAILEY

For your warrior-like efforts to save lives by
increasing awareness of the importance of organ
donation. With love and gratitude, until we meet again.

CARRIE: TO MY SOUL SISTER SANDRA O'HARA

For sharing your phenomenal gifts so tirelessly
and selflessly, which served to open the world of Spirit
to me, reconnecting me with Todd.
Our souls are forever one.

TABLE OF CONTENTS

PREFACE

Miracles are not just something I believe in; I rely upon them. I believe that they happen all the time, to each one of us, it's just a matter of having an open heart and mind, trusting, and recognizing them as such. This is a story about miracles, about the strength of free will, the power of the mind to overcome physical and emotional challenges, and about the power of love. It's one man's extraordinary journey through a series of phenomenal challenges and miraculous events, each one integral to the fact that he's alive, and thriving, today.

— Carrie Meehan

INTRODUCTION

☙

Some days are really special. Todd Hensel received a multivisceral transplant 14 years ago!! After 5 cardiac arrests and many many challenges he survived a 6 organ transplant.* His heart stopped twice during the transplant and we were able to bring him back. One of the most challenging cases of my career. I can't describe the pleasure of seeing him doing so well. Today he drove down with Carrie to see me after many years. Living life the way he envisioned. Being good and doing good. I can only thank God for allowing me to be part of this. A real miracle man!

— Rodrigo Vianna, MD
January 15, 2023
Miami Transplant Institute, Florida

*The spleen is used to transport the pancreas, but is not considered a "billable organ" by insurance companies as it is not vital for survival.

Carrie and Todd met
in high school in 1976

CHAPTER 1
OUR BEGINNING

୬

OUR RELATIONSHIP BACK THEN WAS LOVELY, INNOCENT, AND PURE. I FELT IN MY HEART THAT HE WAS THE MOST BEAUTIFUL SOUL I HAD EVER MET, AND I WAS FIERCELY ATTRACTED TO HIM.

My story with this amazing man, Todd Hensel, began in 1976 when we were in high school together in Michigan. He was my first boyfriend. The thing I notice first about someone, and the thing I am always drawn to about a person, is the way they carry themselves. I believe it speaks volumes about how they feel about themselves. I will never forget the first time I saw Todd walking down the hallway at school. How in the world anyone at that young age could be so grounded, so sure of himself, knowing who he was and what he brought, in a quietly assured way, was beyond me. I was in awe of it then, and I still am. Todd still walks exactly like he did back in high school, and my heart still jumps when I see him.

My Miracle Man

Our relationship back then was lovely, innocent, and pure. I felt in my heart that he was the most beautiful soul I had ever met, and I was fiercely attracted to him.

The problem was I had no idea who I was. I just always felt a bit like an outsider and an observer of life, and I had no idea what my role was meant to be. And for some reason I felt I needed to go away to figure it all out.

I left Michigan in 1989 for the west coast, then much of my adult life was spent in California, Ireland, and France. In the fall of 2008, I was living in Ireland when I heard that Todd was in the hospital. I was told he was struggling with something quite rare that came on suddenly, and he was fighting for his life.

What Todd went through back in 2008-2009 was the result of Methylenetetrahydrofolate reductase (MTHFR), a serious clotting disorder. Todd believes a lethal cocktail of undiagnosed MTHFR and the consumption of part of an energy drink immediately before extreme exercise caused him to develop a series of deadly blood clots. The staggering result was multiple organ failure as the blood clots caused seven of his organs to die, all at once. Ultimately, he was the first man of his age to undergo surgery to receive seven organs from a single donor at one time: stomach, small intestines, large intestines, kidney, liver, pancreas, and spleen (though the spleen was subsequently removed). The surgery took two days to complete. His heart stopped three times during his transplant operation. He also died once before and once following his surgeries, and he recalls vividly what transpired during those times he was clinically "dead." Todd's life-threatening illness opened up a window to the world of Spirit. He was able to see things that most others cannot. Ultimately, he was given more than the gift of life; he was seeing and communicating with Spirits. And that's what brought us back together in 2016.

Carrie and Todd

CHAPTER 2
RECONNECTING

❧

ONE OF THE MOST IMPORTANT BENEFITS I GLEANED FROM THESE YEARS HAS BEEN A RATHER SEAMLESS BLENDING OF LIVING MY LIFE WITH THE EVER-PRESENT ASSISTANCE FROM SPIRIT.

When I moved away from Michigan in 1989, I really did not see myself living there again. It was a great place to grow up, but my sense of adventure was greater than my desire to stay where I was raised, and I wanted to experience as much of the world as I could. To me that meant setting up home in lots of different places. Most of my family was still in Michigan so I knew I'd visit often; for some reason I just felt that to figure out who I was I needed to get away from all that was familiar. (Now I feel a bit like Dorothy from the Wizard of Oz, one of my many life lessons being everything we need is right inside of us... but I still thoroughly appreciate all the adventures anyway!)

Southern California didn't cut it for me, but I adored San Francisco – it reminded me of a smaller Paris. I spent seven years in the bay area working and going to law school, before moving to Ireland to raise a family in 1997, spending a lot of time in France as well. A return to California in 2009 was followed by an unexpected (and fortuitous) move back to Michigan in 2016, which was when Todd and I reconnected.

While I was living in Ireland, I had the tremendous fortune of meeting and working with Sandra O'Hara, my soul sister and most gifted psychic medium (Sandra had the gift of being able to communicate with departed loved ones). Sandra helped me immeasurably in dealing with the loss of my Mum; I found the healing benefit from a session with Sandra to be unparalleled.

Family and friends who came to visit me in Ireland all wanted to have a reading with her. I wanted to help Sandra to reach more people, so when I asked her if she had ever considered holding group events rather than exclusively individual readings, she told me that if I built it, she would come. And so that's precisely what we did. In 2005, I started organizing group events in our little town in Ireland ranging in size from as few as 10 to as many as 50.

When I moved back to California in 2009, Sandra visited me several times each year for group events I had organized all over northern California. I began by simply hanging handmade flyers around town and we started with a group of 25, within a year we had groups with hundreds in attendance. Throughout my many years of organizing events for Sandra, one of the many blessings I received was a profound level of comfort in Spirit interaction. When I use the term "Spirit," I am referring to souls without a physical body, usually departed loved ones. One of the most important benefits I gleaned from these years has been a rather seamless blending of living my life with the ever-present assistance from Spirit. Every home I've lived in has had Spirit activity; each one a positive (or at least learning) experience. I have found the veil between physical and Spirit to be quite thin, once we have the eye and heart to see and listen, and we are open and patient. This chapter in my life was an essential precursor to my reconnection with Todd years later.

Once I was back in Michigan in 2016, I heard from my best childhood friend (who had remained in touch with Todd over the years) that he may be reaching out to me for support with the increased Spirit activity he had been dealing with since his surgery, which was wreaking havoc on his sleep. One July morning as I was standing in my kitchen in northern Michigan, I received a message from Todd. He had seen some of the posts I'd put out on social media related to mediumship events with Sandra, and he wondered if I might be interested in helping him gain some control over the Spirit activity he was experiencing. He recognized it was a gift and he wanted to learn to use it as such, but he wanted to control visiting hours. We talked for a long time on the phone, and he told me his amazing story.

Even as a child, Todd was connected to nature and open to Spirit. He spent hours by himself in his neighborhood nature center, climbing trees and just enjoying being in the outdoors. He always had an awareness that he was not alone, and that gave him a sense of calm and belonging. But after his surgery, Todd's awareness of and interaction with the world of Spirit increased greatly, and as Spirit has no concept of time, it often interrupted his sleep. For example, he would be sleeping in his home, alone, with his service dog Skip, and be woken by Skip barking at lights flashing on and off, or by a drastic cold breeze sweeping through his bedroom. It's important to point out that Skip is a registered service dog, whose sole purpose is to help Todd and who is trained to never react unless he perceives something is a potential threat to Todd. Part of his training actually included being exposed to busy traffic intersections and/or train tracks when he was a puppy, to assess his reactiveness to extreme stimuli.

When Spirit wants to connect with human beings, the most efficient way is when a human's mind is not otherwise occupied with details related to everyday life: in other words, when a person is asleep. Todd was being woken up regularly by Skip barking, lights flashing, and cold temperatures, because his usually busy mind was in a deep restful state. Todd's most vivid experiences with Spirit began while he was in the hospital when he could not tell the difference between a human being and a Spirit. He knew these were folks who had passed while they were in the hospital and wanted to connect with someone that they knew could see them. Spirit knows when a person has died (and returns to life) and knows that they have heightened abilities to see and connect with Spirit. After he went home, in time the vivid nature of these Spirit interactions softened, and the Spirits took on an appearance of orbs or shadows. Some of the most profound experiences we can have are not easily described in words, and Spirit interaction is as profound as it gets. Sometimes Todd was sleeping and would be woken by a sense that he wasn't alone, and then he'd see orbs dancing around his room. Sometimes he'd be in nature, and would see shadows or a shimmery type of energy moving across his field of vision. And while these experiences did not cause him to be afraid, he wanted to stop them from interrupting his sleep, and, if possible, understand how he might be of service to them.

As Todd and I spoke, I realized it was the first time we had spoken in 40 years, yet it felt more comfortable and natural than ever. Perhaps our love story needed those intervening years, with all our respective individual experiences and challenges, to reach its fullest realization and potential. I do believe it was a relief for Todd to reconnect with someone who was familiar to him, and comfortable with things of that nature, and maybe who could help him figure out how to use his gift in an elevated way. We arranged to meet in person the following week. And when I saw him walk across the parking lot toward me that day, my heart leapt just like it used to in high school.

As I was driving to our designated meeting place (which was very close to the high school we attended in Waterford, Michigan), I remember passing by a cemetery on the road and asking myself why I had never noticed it when I was growing up. Bizarre as it may sound, I LOVE cemeteries. Not from the standpoint of visiting the graves of departed loved ones (which I actually never do), but I find them peaceful to go and just be. I enjoy reading headstones and tying families together, imagining or creating their stories in my mind. Anyway, the restaurant at which we planned to meet was not yet open, so Todd suggested that we go to a cemetery he knew of to sit and talk, which of course turned out to be that very cemetery I noticed for the first time earlier that afternoon. As I am a huge believer in the importance of synchronicity, the significance of this was not lost on me.

Sitting under a large oak tree in that cemetery that afternoon talking with Todd, I had the distinct feeling that while I thought I had a fairly good idea of what my life was going to look like, the Universe had something completely different in mind.

Todd tends to measure most events in his life against the backdrop of various hunting seasons

CHAPTER 3
TODD'S STORY

☙

HOWEVER, EARLY THE NEXT MORNING, THE PAIN WAS
SO UNBEARABLE THAT HE INSTEAD DROVE HIMSELF TO AN
URGENT CARE FACILITY NEAR HIS HOME IN MICHIGAN
AND PASSED OUT IN THE DOORWAY FROM THE PAIN.

Todd's extremely diverse range of careers after graduating high school began with time spent in Ohio at a welding school, then on to Texas for several years where he worked in construction, bartending, marketing research and retail management. He returned to Michigan in his mid-twenties, by which time he was working in automotive, then landscaping, and raising his young son Josh on his own. By his early thirties, he had gotten married and had two young children, Jacklyn and Jarod. He worked as a firefighter and a realtor before becoming a licensed plumber, where he first worked for himself and then for a university in Michigan. One of the things we share is an adventurous spirit and a strong desire for as many diverse experiences as our lives can hold.

His health ordeal began on August 29, 2008, when he had been exercising rigorously and regularly, and was in the best shape of his life. He regularly participated in a spinning class, which meant an hour of non-stop giving it his all, having to place towels under his bike to catch all the sweat pouring off his body. Before this particular class, he drank about 1/3 of an energy drink, and within hours after the class he started experiencing cramping in his abdomen.

Todd has a very high pain threshold. He went to bed to try to sleep, planning to go up to his cabin the next morning with his young son, Jarod, for the opening of goose season on September 1 (Todd tends to measure most events in his life against the backdrop of various hunting seasons).

However, early the next morning, the pain was so unbearable that he instead drove himself to an urgent care facility near his home in Michigan and passed out in the doorway from the pain. The staff there recognized that he needed a higher level of care, so an ambulance was arranged to take him to a nearby hospital. The first hospital Todd was taken to didn't know what to do with him, and so they did nothing. For three days. Nothing. Todd's stomach was protruding extensively, and he was in such extreme pain that his body flipped out of bed, and he went unconscious. Finally, after three days, they decided to open him up, only to discover that all the organs in his abdomen had died. They knew they couldn't do anything for Todd and that he needed an even higher level of critical care, so they closed him up and transported him to yet another hospital —Henry Ford Hospital in Dearborn, Michigan—in hopes that their expertise would better serve Todd.

Todd and Blazer

My Miracle Man

CHAPTER 4
"OH SHIT, I DIED"

⤝

TODD'S ATTENTION THEN WENT TO THE WARM FEELING AT HIS BACK AND HE REALIZED HOW GOOD HE FELT — LIKE HE WAS 27 AGAIN, STRONG AS COULD BE, AND HE FELT THE GLOW OF ENERGY AND LIGHT CONTINUE TO SURROUND HIM. HE STARTED FLOATING CLOSER TO THAT ENERGY, PAYING ATTENTION TO THE FEELING OF WARMTH AND LOVE, AND HE CONTINUED TO FEEL BETTER AND BETTER.

The doctors at Henry Ford Hospital operated on Todd and discovered blood clots in his portal vein that had caused the death of his organs, but they also realized that they did not have the expertise to do anything for him. Todd needed an entire new set of organs, and at the time, Michigan didn't perform transplants involving more than one organ, known as multi-visceral transplant surgeries. Whether a state can or cannot offer multi-visceral transplant surgeries is determined by the availability of a surgeon within that state with the requisite training and skill. No discussion took place about the fact that a nearby state actually did have the ability to perform them.

Immediately following that initial operation at Henry Ford, Todd flat-lined for the first time. The medical team was pumping on his heart, repeatedly shocking him, to no avail. Todd remembers floating up through the hospital lights he had been looking up at, hovering there, looking down at the doctors who were debating the time of death. He observed one doctor asking the other what time he thought Todd had died, and the other asking what time they had called it. He also watched as three nurses counted the medical instruments, standing at a table full of bloody tools, calling out each instrument and checking them off a list. He felt a connection to the body he saw lying on the table, but he did not immediately realize it was his own body because he couldn't see his face. He thought maybe it belonged to one of his children. He saw the anesthesiologist, who was someone Todd knew from church, leaning over his head, still not understanding that it was his body. Todd realized that those nurses and doctors were completely unaware of his presence, yet he could see and hear everything they were doing and saying.

Just then he felt a warm, loving presence at his back, though he also somehow was aware that he didn't have a back. It was such a loving and warm presence, and he thought about how wonderful it felt. But he was much more interested in what was going on below, so he kept watching what was taking place in the operating room. The anesthesiologist was leaning over Todd's face, touching him, and Todd knew that he was whispering prayers into his ear (though he couldn't hear them). Just then the anesthesiologist stood up, and that was when Todd saw his own face and realized it was his body lying on that gurney below. He remembers exclaiming, "Oh shit, I died!"

Todd's attention then went to the warm feeling at his back and he realized how good he felt - like he was 27 again, strong as could be, and he felt the glow of energy and light continue to surround him. He started floating closer to that energy, paying attention to the feeling of warmth and love, and he continued to feel better and better. He then heard a voice that he knew to be the Holy Spirit tell him, "Sometimes, even in death, we have free will." Todd knew in his soul that he was communicating with the Holy Spirit, which he understood to be representing God. Todd asked what that meant, to which the Holy Spirit responded, "If you want to go back, you can, but know you will have many days of great pain." It's important to note that this conversation was taking place telepathically, without spoken words. Todd responded that he did have young children and asked if it would be selfish of him to stay, because he felt so good. The Holy Spirit said, "Of course, but again, you have free will." Todd thought about it and asked what he had to do to get back to his body. "Say the Lord's Prayer," the Holy Spirit responded. Todd started to say the Lord's Prayer, and the Holy Spirit told him, "In your greatest days of pain, focus on your Savior on the cross." Todd promised to do so, and as he continued saying the Lord's Prayer, he began getting control over his essence and lowered back down towards his body. When he was about two feet above his body, he could still feel the energy around him; he blinked and then was back in his body looking up.

Todd immediately sat straight up on the operating table and was looking around the operating room. The anesthesiologist shouted to the doctors, "He's back, he's back!" He later told Todd that he had injected enough anesthesia in him to "drop a Clydesdale," but as Todd was still flexing his muscles, the anesthesiologist pumped more into him, along with Propofol, to try to knock him out. The anesthesiologist went around to Todd's back, placed one hand on his forehead and the other on his back, told Todd to not fight him and to lie back down. Unfortunately, he also told Todd not to look down —and of course, that's precisely what Todd then felt compelled to do —and he saw that he was cut open from his breastbone down to his pubic bone, his intestines hanging out, and all his abdominal organs black. The other doctors came running over to Todd in disbelief; Todd remembers seeing the anesthesiologist push the needle administering additional Propofol into his system, and he fell asleep. He had been gone for eleven minutes.

In a conversation Todd had with the anesthesiologist much later, he shared with Todd that this experience had changed his life forever, for the better. He told Todd that it felt like he had touched his soul; he felt Todd's essence pierce through his system as Todd re-entered his body, which had never happened before. He felt Todd's love, innocence, and goodness, and he told Todd that his whole perspective on life and what mattered had been forever altered. After this blessing, which he knew he needed in his life, he told Todd that he took nothing for granted, and he viewed each human being he encountered with reverence, as the sacred soul that they are. In that same conversation afterward, he also told Todd that it was considered a medical impossibility for Todd to be able to sit straight up given the amount of anesthesia and Propofol he had been given (not to mention being cut open from breastbone to pubic bone). That he was awake, aware, and alert was even more incomprehensible. The pain he was in and the surgery they performed necessitated an extraordinarily high dose of anesthesia, which should have rendered him incapable of even moving, much less sitting all the way up in a mentally alert state.

Following this initial surgery, the doctors at Henry Ford realized that there was nothing that they could do for Todd, because Michigan did not perform multi-visceral operations at the time. There was no established network between states for placing a patient where a multi-organ transplant could be performed. The patient's life was quite literally dependent upon the skill set available within the geographical state boundaries. A hospital in Michigan could not save his life, and so, the doctors at Henry Ford Hospital placed him in hospice.

Todd and Iris

Todd and Josh

Chapter 5
Visit Of Little Boy From Spirit

❧

She shared that she had felt her little boy's presence with her all day that day, right down to feeling him tugging at her scrubs.

Several days later, Todd recalls one of the nurses came into his room with a little boy. He noticed the little boy was wearing a puffy blue jacket and a red hat, and he was holding onto the nurse's scrubs, smiling and waving at Todd. Todd presumed it must have been a day at the hospital where staff could bring their children to work with them. The nurse was talking to Todd and taking his vitals, all the while Todd was looking at her little boy. The nurse then turned to walk out; as she got to the door, the little boy, still holding onto her scrubs, turned and smiled and waved at Todd.

Two hours later, when that same nurse came to take Todd's vitals again, the little boy was not with her. Todd asked her where her little boy had gone, and the nurse asked what he was talking about. Todd explained that the first time she had come into his room, he had seen her little boy with the blue puffy jacket and the red hat, holding onto her scrubs. The nurse burst into tears and said, "It was one year ago today that he was hit by a truck and killed while he waited at the bus stop. That's what he was wearing." She then left the room, very upset. About an hour later, she returned, and apologized to Todd. She shared that she had felt her little boy's presence with her all day that day, right down to feeling him tugging at her scrubs. Todd told her that he definitely was with her, that Todd had seen him, and that he was happy, smiling and waving.

This was the first of many instances of Todd seeing Spirits in 3-D, as I like to describe it, which is simply to say that they appeared as realistic visually to Todd as the human beings they were visiting. The hospital is an especially busy place for Spirit activity, as Todd soon came to realize.

My Miracle Man

CHAPTER 6
THE BUSH PILOT

∾

HE RECALLS THE PILOT SCREAMING OBSCENITIES AT THE HOSPITAL'S MEDICAL STAFF WHO UNHOOKED TODD FROM ALL THE LINES FEEDING HIM PAIN MEDS BEFORE PLACING HIM IN THE AIRPLANE, TURNING AROUND TO PLACE HIS HAND ON TODD'S SHOULDER, BEGGING HIM TO PLEASE NOT DIE IN HIS PLANE.

Todd's eldest son, Josh, was 22 years old at the time and had also recently lost his mother. After the doctors at Henry Ford Hospital told Josh that his father may die within hours or days, he fell to the floor and was wailing at the foot of Todd's bed. A visiting surgeon, Dr. Rodrigo Vianna, walked by. Upon hearing Josh sobbing, he felt compelled to turn around and walk into Todd's room and read his chart. He asked if Todd was Josh's father, and when Josh said he was, Dr. Vianna told Josh that Todd would certainly die if he stayed in Michigan. Dr. Vianna was visiting from Indiana University Hospital to advocate for multi-visceral transplants. He told Josh that he knew he may be able to save Todd's life, but Josh needed to find a way to get Todd to Indiana University. Dr. Vianna's hands were tied. He had no medical authority at Henry Ford Hospital, so it would fall to Todd's 22-year-old son to find a way to transport Todd to Indiana.

Josh jumped up in renewed hope and ran out to the nurses' station. Josh had had a strong impact on the nurses at the hospital, capturing their hearts with his pure, passionate love and presence. Unfortunately, because Todd had been placed in hospice, he was denied a life flight. Josh was undeterred, and he begged and pleaded with the nurses until he convinced them to help him find a way to get his dad to IU.

Together, miraculously, they were able to locate a private bush pilot who had been in Newfoundland on a caribou hunt, was flying a cargo plane out west to Colorado to go elk hunting and would be stopping at an airport in Detroit on the way (I believe this man was an angel with a different set of wings). This beautiful stranger agreed to stop to pick Todd up and fly him to IU.

Todd has been an avid hunter since he was 14 years old and he remembers that flight well —which is a miracle in and of itself since he was strapped to a gurney, his abdomen partially open, internal organs dead, not connected to any pain meds whatsoever, his body bucking from the shock and pain, continually passing out. He recalls the pilot screaming obscenities at the hospital's medical staff who unhooked Todd from all the lines feeding him pain meds before placing him in the airplane, turning around to place his hand on Todd's shoulder, begging him to please not die in his plane. Todd was gasping and fighting for his life, but he told the pilot not to worry, he wasn't dying that day. He remembers looking around that plane, seeing the pilot's guns and hunting gear, and thinking that one day he would love to go on an elk hunt (which he has done twice since 2008).

The level of pain Todd was experiencing during that plane ride was unimaginable; he could not control his body's continual bucking from the extreme pain. To this day, I marvel when he describes the experience: he refers to things happening to "my body," not to "me." Todd just really gets that we are not our bodies! This awareness, which he has always had, absolutely played a pivotal role in his ability to take control of his attention and focus it elsewhere during his days of most extreme pain, thereby helping him to get through it all and heal. He has the strongest mind of anyone I know, and an innate understanding of the power of that strength in the ability to overcome physical pain.

CHAPTER 7
INDIANA UNIVERSITY
– ONE DAY AT A TIME

༈

IT IS IMPOSSIBLE TO OVEREMPHASIZE THE MIRACLE OF TODD CATCHING THE EYE OF DR. VIANNA, ONE OF PERHAPS A HANDFUL OF SURGEONS IN THE COUNTRY WHO HAD THE KNOWLEDGE, SKILLS, INSTITUTIONAL BACKING AND SHEER CHUTZPAH TO PERFORM THE MULTI-VISCERAL TRANSPLANT.

The bush pilot successfully delivered Todd to IU (though they initially landed at the wrong airport and had to take off and land a second time closer to the hospital in Indianapolis). Then began the unimaginable struggle of staying healthy and strong enough to remain on the transplant list and be able to undergo an unprecedented transplant of this magnitude, all the while unsure as to whether the organs would even become available.

The surgical team, led by Dr. Vianna, removed all of Todd's abdominal organs and had him connected to machines to keep him alive, with dozens of hanging bags of fluids and medicine attached and four pick lines in him. They gave him a tracheotomy, so they would be able to provide him with life-saving oxygen if needed.

Todd was at Indiana University Hospital for over two months before his ultimate surgery, which took place over the course of two days, November 14-15, 2008. He went from weighing 225 pounds (of solid muscle and in peak condition) down to 100 pounds when he ultimately went into surgery. Indiana University's doctors had done thorough examinations on him and determined that he had a strong and healthy heart, lungs, and equally important, mind.

It is impossible to overemphasize the miracle of Todd catching the eye of Dr. Vianna, one of perhaps a handful of surgeons in the country who had the knowledge, skills, institutional backing and sheer chutzpah to perform the multi-visceral transplant Todd needed. Multi-visceral transplantation was not well known (and still isn't), even among physicians. Dr. Vianna recently shared with us that "everyone thought [he] was crazy to accept Todd [as a patient]," but he told Todd that he knew when he first met him in Michigan, Todd had what it would take to make it through an operation of this magnitude, physically and mentally. Dr. Vianna had never performed such a surgery before, but he knew that as a team he and Todd would be successful. Todd showed no evidence of cholesterol or heart disease ordinarily associated with someone 48 years old, because he exercised, was always in top physical condition, seldom consumed processed foods, and primarily ate only meat and fish he harvested himself (therefore free from hormones or antibiotics).

Then came the challenge of dealing with the insurance company. Todd's career had been as a licensed plumber at Oakland University in Rochester, Michigan. Fortuitously (but not coincidentally), one year before in the fall of 2007, when he was presented with the annual opportunity to modify his coverage, Todd recalls having had an overwhelming gut feeling to take the unlimited medical coverage. It only cost an additional ten dollars per month, which he figured was the equivalent of a couple cups of coffee a week (coffee is very important to Todd, it makes perfect sense to me that he measured this decision against it). He remembers that someone from the human resource department at the university had called to ask him if he was sure that he wanted that level of coverage, because no one at the university had ever opted for it before, and it would entail additional paperwork to do this for him. He always trusted his instincts and responded with an unequivocal "yes."

Now that he was at Indiana University and deemed strong and healthy enough by doctors there, the insurance company didn't want to pay for the surgery, so they sent their own doctor to IU to attempt to prove that Todd wasn't healthy or strong enough to live through it. To their dismay, all the tests continued to show the same thing: no evidence of any weakness or disease whatsoever, in fact Todd possessed formidable strength of body, mind, and spirit. They were therefore unable to deny funding the surgery.

Todd spent several weeks leading up to the surgery in a medically induced coma. Then, in early November Todd became septic. On Monday, November 10, the doctors came in and woke Todd up to tell him that if he remained septic, he would never make it through surgery. They would have to take him off the transplant list and Todd's condition would worsen. And if he wasn't healthy enough for the transplant, he would die. The life-support machines were only prolonging the inevitable. The doctors discussed the removal of the life support machines and essentially asked Todd to pick a day to die. Always beyond thoughtful, Todd chose Thursday so as not to ruin anybody's weekend. They then asked him how he wanted to go—awake or asleep? Of course, Todd wanted to be awake. They asked him why, and he recalls telling them that "You only die once, and I want to feel it all in a fully aware state. It's just pain and it's going to end." They called in the hospital psychiatrist to evaluate Todd to ensure he was of sound mind to make such a decision, which, of course, he was.

Todd and Skip

Todd and Skip

CHAPTER 8
CHILDLIKE FAITH

❧

TODD ASKED, "WHY ME? WHY AM I BLESSED WITH YOUR PRESENCE?" THE HOLY SPIRIT RESPONDED, "WHY NOT YOU?" TODD ANSWERED, "BECAUSE I'M JUST A PLUMBER, I WORK WITH MY HANDS." THE HOLY SPIRIT THEN SAID, "WELL, YOUR SAVIOR WAS A CARPENTER WHO WORKED WITH HIS HANDS."

On Wednesday, November 12, 2008, the doctors came in to wake Todd up to remind him that in accordance with his request to die on a Thursday, they would be unplugging him from everything the next day, but they wanted to draw one last set of bloodwork. They told him that they may be taking him off the transplant list because he was extremely septic. They drew his blood, and Todd asked them to please let him stay awake. It was 10:30 in the morning; the doctors left Todd alone in his room.

Todd then surrendered his whole Spirit, released all anxiety, and began talking to God, professing his love, and inviting God to take him then. Once Todd got into a state of what he calls "childlike faith," which he understands to be a state of pure, zen-like absolute faith, with no doubt whatsoever, the Holy Spirit appeared. All of Todd's pain disappeared and he found himself in a state of euphoria and pure bliss. Todd asked, "Why me? Why am I blessed with Your presence?" The Holy Spirit responded, "Why not you?" Todd answered, "Because I'm just a plumber, I work with my hands." The Holy Spirit then said, "Well, your Savior was a carpenter who worked with His hands." Todd went into deep thought on this, and the Holy Spirit continued, "All through life, you have free will. And, so, it is up to you." Todd confirmed again with the Holy Spirit that he did want to live, and the Holy Spirit reminded him, "In your worst days of pain, focus on your Savior on the cross, let that be your focus." Todd promised that he would do so. The Holy Spirit then retreated.

Just then three IU doctors returned to Todd's room. They could feel that something had happened in the room, and they were asking, "What happened in here?" They could feel there had been an energy shift. They called the nurses in and demanded of them, "What happened in here? Who gave him something? What did you give him?" The nurses responded that they hadn't given Todd anything. The doctors were angry and were insisting that someone must have given Todd something. One of the doctors then demanded that they draw another set of bloodwork immediately and get it down to the lab. The doctors were looking at the machines and noted that Todd's vitals looked good; Todd heard one of them say that if the bloodwork came back good then he could return to the transplant list.

When the bloodwork results were returned from the lab, it was revealed that Todd's sepsis had completely disappeared. The doctors said, "We don't know what happened, but you're back on the transplant list for today." Todd knew what had happened: he'd been blessed by the Holy Spirit's visit. The doctors could feel that the energy had shifted, but they didn't understand it. And so, they left, but they returned that evening, telling Todd that he would still be unplugged from the machines the next day as had been planned. They were certain that donor organs would not become available in time for Todd to be well enough for surgery. He was, after all, living only because of life-support machines and his condition would continue to deteriorate. But because his bloodwork results matched pre-established parameters, he was back on the transplant list. Todd knew that he had just experienced another miracle. What he didn't know was that there were more to follow. The medical staff put him back into an induced coma and left the room.

The doctors returned the following night and brought Todd out of the coma. They told him that they had found a donor, and to prepare himself for the surgery. Dr. Vianna then came in, took one of Todd's hands in his own, put his other hand on Todd's cheek, and told Todd that he needed Todd to fight, to fight and never give up. He told Todd that he knew he could perform the surgery, but that they were a team and that in order for this to work, they needed to do it together. Todd gave him a nod.

The surgery spanned the course of two days, November 14-15, 2008. Todd drained the hospital's blood bank, using 115 units of blood through the surgery.

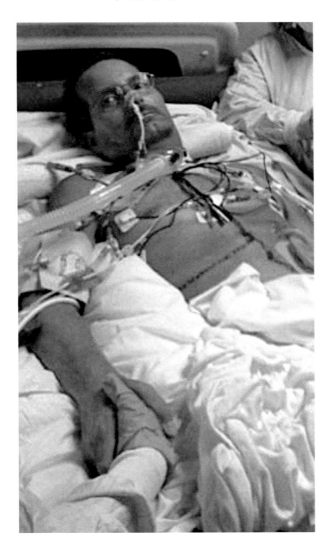

Another day on the farm

CHAPTER 9
A VISIT FROM A FALLEN ANGEL

***

AS HE LOOKED BACK AT HIS BODY, HE SAW HIS NURSE SITTING ON TOP OF HIM, HER LEGS ON EITHER SIDE OF HIM, PUMPING ON HIS HEART, SWEATING, CRYING, AND SHOUTING AT HIM, "DON'T QUIT!"

After waking up from surgery, Todd was unable to fall back asleep. It hurt so much to breathe that for two days afterward, he was not able to sleep. Every time he would start to fall asleep, he would stop breathing, and then his body would jerk, and he would wake up. He was not able to speak because of the tracheotomy, and he couldn't move because of all the IVs and pick lines going into him.

Nurses switched in and out because it was so emotionally difficult for them to spend too much time with Todd. On the second day following surgery, his main nurse had returned to take care of him. Todd was awake and saw what he thought was a beautiful angel in white who kept coming to visit him. She was the most beautiful vision of a female Todd had ever seen, with long flowing blonde hair, and she told him clearly, "Just stop breathing and all of your pain will go away." Finally, Todd thought that this must be God telling him it was time to let go, so he took one last breath and then floated out of his body again. He then turned to look for the angel in white, but she was nowhere to be seen. Todd could see the familiar glow outside of the window and felt his soul drawn to the glow, so he began floating over toward the window. There were photos of his children on the wall next to the window that the nurses had taped there weeks before. He looked at those photos. Just then the Holy Spirit appeared and told him, "If you go through the window, you're not coming back. If you go into the light, Todd, you are not coming back." Todd paused. The Holy Spirit reminded Todd of free will. Todd asked, "Is it the Our Fathers?" The Holy Spirit responded, "Yes."

Todd floated there for a bit before beginning to say the Lord's Prayer. As he looked back at his body, he saw his nurse sitting on top of him, her legs on either side of him, pumping on his heart, sweating, crying, and shouting at him, "Don't quit! Don't give up! Your kids are here, and they need you!" He had been gone for between eight and ten minutes. Todd was so struck by how hard she was working on his body, pumping on his heart, reaching over and hitting a buzzer that was making a loud noise. Sweat and tears fell from her onto him. Todd looked at his lifeless body, flopping when she pumped on him, and every time she did so, he saw on the machine that his heart rate jumped up. This went on for several minutes.

Todd then started saying the Lord's Prayer and began floating over toward his body. The experience was the same as the first time: when he was directly over his body, it felt like he blinked and was back in his body, looking up at her. Once he was able to focus on her, she screamed, "You're back! You're back! Don't quit! Don't give up! You keep fighting!" She grabbed his face and then kept pumping his heart. A medical team then ran into the room and began working on him, sticking needles into him, but Todd could feel nothing. He felt that his body was in a completely different state after being gone.

The nurse realized that something was wrong, she knew intuitively that they were all missing something essential. She asked him a lot of questions trying to figure out what it was. "Are you not sleeping? Have you not slept?"

she asked. Todd's ability to communicate was limited to blinking his eyes to indicate "yes" in response to a question; he could also communicate rudimental words by using his eyes to point to large letters on a clipboard. Todd was blinking at her trying to communicate his response. Then she asked, "Are you having a hard time breathing?" Todd quickly blinked at her in response. The nurse then knew that he needed to be on a ventilator. The doctors were debating whether to put him on one, the nurse insisted that it had to happen because she knew that Todd couldn't breathe, and therefore couldn't sleep. As soon as they hooked Todd up to the ventilator, one breath and he felt his body relax. By the second or third breath, he fell asleep.

Todd later learned that at this very same time, a neighbor friend of his back in Michigan who was quite religious had been reading a bible passage about an angel of light immediately following Todd's surgery. This friend had a dream of this angel of light visiting Todd, and he knew from the bible that it was a fallen angel. He knew he needed to warn Todd about his premonition, and he was so inspired that he drove down to Indianapolis that very day. When he arrived at ICU at Indiana University Hospital, he was told that the previous day Todd had coded. Though he couldn't have a conversation with his neighbor, he felt an overwhelming sense of relief and gratitude that his friend confirmed what he felt and made the six-hour drive to warn him. The angel of light had visited Todd the day before and caused Todd to die the second time. Todd knew that this fallen angel was trying to undo a miracle. But he also knew the Holy Spirit was stronger.

Todd and Josh mending fences

Josh, Jacklyn, Jarod, and Todd

CHAPTER 10
MANY DAYS OF PAIN

~

TODD SOON LEARNED THAT THOSE "MANY DAYS OF GREAT PAIN" TO WHICH THE HOLY SPIRIT REFERRED WENT FAR BEYOND THE PHYSICAL CHALLENGES OF HEALING.

Following that third visit by the Holy Spirit, Todd's healing was a very long, arduous experience. He had to learn to breathe, walk and talk again, along with how to live in a body that often felt foreign to him, and because of the new organs, it was. He often thought of the warning he was given in his first conversation with the Holy Spirit that he would experience many days of extreme pain, but he knew that he had been through the worst, divinely supported, and that each day of physical life is a gift.

In the months immediately following Todd's transplant surgery, the doctors and other medical professionals all advised Todd that life as he knew it would be completely different than it was before his surgery. They encouraged him to get comfortable doing crossword puzzles and watching television. Because his central nervous system was compromised by two and a half months of lying in a hospital bed, open and empty between his ribs and his pelvis, and because of the atrophy his body had suffered, they did not know if he would ever walk again. Within a week after the surgery, with open wounds healing from the inside out in two spots and staples holding his abdomen together, two very strong, muscular, large male nurses came into Todd's room daily to begin the process of sitting, and then standing, him upright. They had tied straps around Todd's chest, thereby connecting all three of them. Blood was falling from his wounds, and the pain of this was so excruciating that Todd would sweat profusely and then continually pass out, because of his new organs shifting inside. Each day, these nurses tried to help Todd take one more step. Initially and for the first several months, Todd could not feel his legs at all, and the messages from his brain were not reaching his legs and feet, so he was completely reliant upon these nurses to hold him upright. However, Todd knew that he didn't just survive all that he had been through to become a Sudoku champ; his response to the doctors was "Just watch me." It was the power of his mind and heart that helped get him that far, and he was determined to live the rest of his life to the fullest.

Todd soon learned that those "many days of great pain" to which the Holy Spirit referred went far beyond the physical challenges of healing, which were tremendous in and of themselves. Throughout Todd's stay at Indiana University Hospital, he was also working with a team of psychiatrists. The concern and expectation were that the level of extreme pain that Todd was suffering would either put him in shock or drive him insane. These psychiatrists also observed the dynamics in Todd's marriage, and they advised him that he would be facing certain divorce, as they observed that his (then) wife had checked out of the marriage. As devastating as this was to hear, Todd was not surprised, because he had felt a distinct lack of compassion from her throughout his entire stay at the hospital. He recalls hospital staff commenting on the infrequency of visits by his wife, and the fact that on one occasion she was even ousted from his room in ICU by his doctor because she had brought food in from a nearby restaurant and was eating in front of him immediately following his surgery, and he hadn't eaten in months.

When he was taken home, the home he had built himself, he was placed in the basement of the home. It was a finished basement, but it was cold, and he was isolated and removed from his entire family, who were either in their bedrooms or in the kitchen and living area one floor above. He could hear them all walking around, talking, laughing, and eating, while he lay there in pain and needing something, too weak to call out, and he would pray and wonder when his nurse would be arriving that day.

He learned upon arriving home that many of his personal effects, clothing, and tools were simply missing; they had been given away while he was in the hospital.

Sure enough, within a year following his return home, he opened his front door one day and found himself face-to-face with a sheriff's deputy and a process server from the court. It is important to note that he still had open wounds, one of which was on his tailbone and required 24-hour a day connection to a wound vacuum, and he was learning to walk again, reliant upon a walker. These men forcibly thrust divorce papers into the front of his body, a direct blow to his stitches, causing him to fall to the ground in pain.

Todd knew that he needed to be as mentally strong, focused, and alert as he could possibly be to fight this next legal battle. Since his release from the hospital, he had been on a very strong pain med regimen so that his body could heal effectively: fentanyl patches and liquid morphine, the dosages of which were being slowly decreased. He recalls the effect of fentanyl patches was to rob him of his memory and cause him to live his life in flashcards. Around this same time, the doctors at IU wanted to send him to a rehab facility to wean him off these medications in the least stressful way to his body. Todd knew he had the ability to do this on his own, so he drove himself up to his cabin in northern Michigan and quit everything, cold turkey. He walked his land for three days, his body sweating profusely and shaking. He just kept walking his land. By the end of the third day, he was free of pain medication and psyched himself up for the next battle.

Thus began an unfathomable roller coaster ride through the impersonal injustices of the legal system. A judge of questionable honor and integrity characterized him as a "distraction" to his family, ordered Todd to leave his home, and mandated that he pay child support, though he was entirely and permanently disabled and could not work.

The psychiatrists were right. Todd learned that his wife had filed for divorce before he came home months earlier while fighting for his life in the hospital.

The one-bullet buck

Chapter 11
One Bullet

❧

There were nights he slept in his truck, there was often uncertainty about where the next meal would come from, but no longer did Todd question whether he should have given in to that fallen angel.

Todd had lost his job, his home, his family, and all visitation with his children. He had lost everything he had fought to live for and was still quite literally fighting for his life one day at a time. All of this felt overwhelming, and he found himself in a dark place emotionally. He questioned whether God had meant for him to live after all, so he took himself to the place he always felt closest to the Divine — nature. He drove up to his land in northern Michigan where he had spent so many days hunting and camping with his children.

A single bullet was in his pocket. His plan was to sit in his deer blind, pray, meditate, and ask God what he was meant to do. Recalling the message of the Holy Spirit, Todd focused on his Savior on the cross, and asked for a sign. One of the many things that I admire and adore about Todd is that when it comes to the bigger questions he ponders, he appreciates the importance of being still and connecting with his higher power, his God, and awaiting his voice of inner knowing telling him what God's desire is.

Hours went by. It was cold, cloudy, misty, and silent in those woods. Todd's eyes were closed for the entire time. When he finished praying, he opened his eyes, and found himself looking directly into the eyes of one of the biggest bucks he had ever seen while hunting. He knew that God had given him his answer. The bullet was not meant for him; he was meant to live. And continue fighting. As painful and unjust as it felt to him at times, knowing that it was God's will that he live gave him the strength to keep fighting. There were nights he slept in his truck, there was often uncertainty about where the next meal would come from, but no longer did Todd question whether he should have given in to that fallen angel.

Dr. Rodrigo Vianna and Todd reunion

CHAPTER 12
THE RIPPLE EFFECT

࿉

THERE ARE NO COINCIDENCES, JUST SYNCHRONICITIES
THAT REMIND US OF THE INTERCONNECTEDNESS OF ALL.

The interconnectedness of all is a truth that continues
to make itself known to me in a myriad of ways the longer
I am alive on this planet. I believe we aren't always given
the gift of seeing explicitly how one thing or one person
impacts another, but when we are, I receive it as validation
from the Divine that there are no accidents, and we really
are (to quote one of my favorite teachers, Ram Dass) just
all "walking each other home."

So, I would like to share a couple of stories of lives
impacted by Todd's experience. About a year and a half
after Todd's surgery, he had a strong feeling that he needed
to go back to one of the hospitals in Michigan he had
been at, before he was transferred to Indiana University
Hospital. Something told him that he needed to do this for
himself as well as for someone else, so one day he popped
in at this particular hospital. As he entered the Intensive

Care Unit of the hospital, several of the nurses recognized him (by his cleft chin, they shared with him). They told him that they remembered him, which is amazing since he was only with them for a few days. They then told him that he needed to meet with one doctor in particular, who was the head of the Critical Care Unit and had been struggling lately. This was the same doctor who had overseen Critical Care during Todd's visit a year and a half before. Todd was taken back through a series of hallways to this doctor's office. As his office door opened, the doctor looked up from his desk and he couldn't keep the shock from his face. He exclaimed, "Oh my God, I know who you are. I never thought I would see you again!" He went on to explain that he had treated thousands of patients throughout his career, and no one had ever come back to see him. He acknowledged that he had not been able to help Todd and presumed that Todd had not survived. He then shared with Todd that he had been questioning his career and had been asking for a sign. He became quiet and then quite emotional for a few minutes. He then held up a piece of paper and said, "Do you know what this is?" Todd responded, "No." The doctor went on to say, "This is my resignation letter. I was going to turn it in today. But here you are, I've got my answer." He then stood up, walked over to his shredder, and placed the letter in it. He knew that Todd was the sign he had been asking for.

The second story is about one life that was saved: a friend of ours is an anesthesiologist and was working at a hospital in northern Michigan a couple of years following Todd's surgery. He was working night shift and learned that another doctor on duty was about to place one of his patients in hospice—a young man who had presented with symptoms that would have required a multi-organ transplant to save his life. Michigan was still a single organ transplant state at the time. Our friend, the anesthesiologist, was in the right place at the right time, learned about this patient, and suggested they reach out to Indiana University Hospital, as IU has the ability to perform multi-organ transplants. That young man was transferred to IU and received the organs he needed to live. This same young man went on to study medicine there at Indiana University! There are no coincidences, just synchronicities that remind us of the interconnectedness of all.

*With our friend Kyle Bailey on our
2018 trip to raise awareness of the
importance of organ donation.*

CHAPTER 13
LIFE'S A JOURNEY

☙

FUNDAMENTAL TO TODD'S LIFE IS HIS UNDERSTANDING THAT WE ARE ALL HERE TO MAKE A POSITIVE DIFFERENCE IN EACH OTHER'S LIVES...

One morning in early 2018, immediately after we moved from Michigan to rural Tennessee to begin a peaceful life of farming, Todd greeted me over morning coffee with, "I think we need to go on a trip with a guy from Michigan who is a four-organ transplant recipient." Our (now) friend Kyle Bailey was planning to ride his bike from Michigan to Florida, meeting with all the organ procurement organizations (OPOs) along the way. His goal was to increase national donor signatures by 500,000. Kyle's friend who was to follow him in an RV was suddenly unable to go, so he needed a driver. Todd knew that his participation would go a long way towards helping Kyle to reach his goal, so we packed Todd's truck up and drove back to Michigan to help support Kyle on this very worthwhile adventure.

This was Todd's way of giving thanks to his donor and his donor's family, as well as raising awareness of the importance of being an organ donor. Along the way, we had the chance to talk to hundreds of people about organ donation. We discovered there is a common fear that being listed as an organ donor could influence a doctor's efforts to save a patient during a medical crisis. The truth is that doctors are oath-bound to do everything possible to save a patient's life. And in fact, very few people die in such a way that their organs can be used for transplantations. According to the United Network for Organ Sharing (UNOS), it's less than 2% of deaths. Typically, only patients who die while on life support have organs that have received sufficient oxygen to be donated.

The trip was a success on many levels. Most importantly, national signatures increased by 500,000, we gained a friend for life (and beyond) in Kyle, and we learned a lot about areas for improvement in the organ donation world. It became clear as we moved from state to state that many more lives will be saved if there is a more cohesive approach, better interstate communication and cooperation, and perhaps more federal attention placed on the importance of organ donation. Too few physicians are aware that multi-visceral transplants are an option for their seriously ill patients. Too few states have hospitals that perform these operations. And if you are lucky enough to be under the care of a physician who knows about multi-visceral transplants, transportation options for patients are spotty at best.

Fundamental to Todd's life is his understanding that we are all here to make a positive difference in each other's lives; life is short, and every moment of every day is precious. To that end, he spends time each day providing support to transplant survivors on social media and through his blog mymiracleman.com.

In 1988, the first year that information was available through the Organ Procurement and Transplant Network website, there were only 38 multi-visceral transplant surgeries performed in the U.S. In 2021, 1,258 of these surgeries were performed, and for the first seven months of 2022, 784 multi-visceral transplant surgeries have been performed in the U.S. [Statistics from optn.transplant. hrsa.gov and U.S. Senate Report dated 08/03/20 "SFC Majority/Minority Health LA/s Hearing."] Sadly, around

6,000 Americans die each year while waiting for organ transplants. Many, like Todd, will be suddenly thrust into the world of transplantation—experiencing a medical crisis they never saw coming and desperately needing the selfless gift of someone they've never met. You, a family member, a dear friend or coworker could find yourself in the same desperate situation. In a world where things are often beyond our control, this is one area where each of us can help. We CAN turn the tide in a positive way. We invite you to look at the list at the end of this book for things you can do to make miracles happen.

Chapter 14
Lean On Me

༜

AND MY HEART OVERFLOWED, AGAIN, WITH LOVE FOR
THIS AMAZING MAN WHO TRULY DOES RESIDE IN A STATE
OF GRACE, GRATITUDE, AND FULL LOVING PRESENCE.

It's now the summer of 2021, and Todd and I share a
beautiful, happy, peaceful life in rural Tennessee, during
a surreal worldwide pandemic, raising grass-fed cattle,
chickens, making CBD oil with the industrial hemp we
grow, and spending a lot of time in nature every day. The
ranch we now call home was neglected for years before we
moved onto it; it has been our primary focus to breathe
life into it and watch it blossom in the most beautiful way,
supporting abundantly the animals who fill it now.

This morning Todd told me how grateful he is for having
insight to be able to appreciate the little things. When I asked
him what he was referring to specifically, he went back to the
time he was lying in a hospital bed twelve years ago, with
so many needles in his body that he could not move, and a
tracheotomy in his neck so he could not speak, in an utterly

reliant state. And there would be moments when he would feel so hot and his face would be sweating and the salt would get in his eyes and sting and he could not ask for help, and he couldn't bring his hand to his eyes to wipe them himself. He remembered feeling such gratitude when a kind nurse would finally realize the discomfort that he was in. Or when he had phlegm in his throat but couldn't clear it and couldn't tell anyone about it, and ultimately his son Jarod, who has always been intuitively connected to Todd beyond words, would realize what was wrong and ask a nurse to swab it for him. He felt nothing but gratitude when these things would happen.

And my heart overflowed, again, with love for this amazing man who truly does reside in a state of grace, gratitude, and full loving presence. He really gets that those little things are truly the really big things, the things that matter most.

We have had five baby calves born on our little farm in the past month. Maybe it isn't a good idea to have favorites, and as I tend to treat our cows like they are our children, I try hard not to. However, that same principle doesn't hold true for the cows' sentiments for people, apparently, because Iris is completely in love with Todd. She could be acres away in the field, but as soon as she hears Todd's voice she will quite literally come running. And if he is walking in the field, she is right beside him, nudging him until he stops to rub her neck.

So, when Iris gave birth to Janis (our current naming theme is musicians, whereas Iris is one of our original four flower girls—Dahlia, Azalea, Rose and Iris) about a month ago, we knew she was excited and proud to show her new baby off to Todd. As he made his way down the steep hill in the back field to pay her an initial visit, he observed about 30 turkey vultures swarming mama and baby. They were quite organized in their attack and were gradually wearing Iris out. Todd was able to shoo several of them away before he scooped the newborn Janis into his arms and carried her up the hill.

Now, this would be challenging for anyone given the weight of a calf and the steep grade of our hills but was especially so for Todd: he is missing that part of his intestines that absorbs iron, because that's how the doctors had to connect them. What this means is that his body doesn't absorb and retain iron like the rest of the population who haven't had a transplant, and that translates to a lower level of oxygen in his blood. He therefore gets winded much quicker than he ever did before. He is still much stronger than most men of any age, but he doesn't have the lung capacity that he used to, so carrying a 65-pound calf up a steep hill in 90-degree weather was a massive endeavor.

Thank God it was Iris' baby, because she not only let Todd pick up her newborn and carry her, but she also sensed how much he was struggling, so she moved her massive body closer to him so that he could lean on her as he walked. The sight of the three of them cresting that hill behind our home was the most magical sight I have ever seen: Todd lovingly carrying Iris's calf to safety and Iris physically supporting Todd, the human she adores. When moments like these happen (and I am grateful and blessed to be able to say that our life is truly filled with such magical moments), I catch my breath and pause to reflect on the miracle of this amazing man with the biggest heart, and strongest will, of anyone I have ever known, and I give thanks for the Divine's role in bringing us back together.

Recently I found my sophomore high school photograph that had my inscription to Todd on the back,

"I hope we stay together forever." After a 40-year hiatus, at long last, we now have forever. Miracles are real.

Todd and Janis,
right after saving her life.

Jarod, Todd, Jacklyn, and Josh

Chapter 15
A Conversation With Dr. Ekser

~

More communication is needed between hospitals, states, and organ procurement organizations (OPOs) to ensure patients get necessary care sooner.

You may be wondering, what has changed or improved in the 15 years since Todd's transplant surgeries? We recently spoke to Dr. Burcin Ekser, Director of Transplant Research at Indiana University. Here are some of the key points from that conversation:

ONGOING CHALLENGES

There is still a lack of awareness. It's not just lay people who aren't aware that intestinal transplants are possible, many physicians are unaware that they are possible! This lack of awareness puts patients at risk by delaying or even eliminating life-saving procedures.

Intestines are the most challenging organ to transplant. Only a few centers in the country perform intestinal transplants, and very few surgeons do them. The training is extensive, and the surgeries themselves are physically challenging and excessively long compared to other organ transplant surgeries. Most medical students opt for less grueling disciplines.

The annual number of intestinal transplant surgeries is decreasing. The type of extensive multi-visceral transplant surgery Todd received in 2008 was rare for its time and may be even more rare today. Lack of awareness on the part of physicians means oftentimes patients are referred very late, compromising the viability of a successful transplant. More communication is needed between hospitals, states, and organ procurement organizations (OPOs) to ensure patients get necessary care sooner. Patients in need of transplants die unnecessarily if they have the misfortune of finding themselves in a hospital that doesn't perform the needed surgery and their medical team doesn't understand the requisite transplant might be available elsewhere. Much more communication is needed between states.

IMPROVEMENTS IN THE SCIENCE

TECHNOLOGY HAS ADVANCED. When Todd's organs died in August 2008, the hospitals did exploratory surgery and saw that his portal vein had clots. Imaging and CT scans have improved in the past 15 years such that physicians can locate a clot much quicker and sometimes open/ dissolve/ remove it. This can prevent the need to perform a transplant on the organ affected by a blood clot, which also has some bearing on the decrease in intestinal transplants.

IT'S A DOUBLE-EDGED SWORD. The advancements in science and technology translate to a greater ability to perform more, and more types, of transplant surgeries. But there is still a massive shortage of organs, due to a lack of public awareness as well as misconceptions and fear regarding being an organ donor.

MAKING MIRACLES
– A CALL TO ACTION

There are many ways you can help pave the path for better transplant care in the U.S. You never know if the life that will be saved is your own or maybe the life of a family member. Below are some of the most powerful things you can do and links to more information.

SIGN UP AS AN ORGAN DONOR. One donor can save EIGHT lives, and you can easily sign up at optn.transplant.hrsa. gov. Also, speak with your family and friends about signing up. It's one of the most effective ways to make a difference.

WRITE TO YOUR STATE REPRESENTATIVES. Send an email or letter to your state representatives (senate.gov) and ask for more attention to be placed on ensuring proper oversight of the OPOs and the OPTN There is a sample email on Todd's blog https://mymiracleman.com that gives all of the pertinent information.

DONATE OR VOLUNTEER WITH ORGANIZATIONS LIKE ANGEL FLIGHT. Angel Flight is a nonprofit organization that offers free flights for transplant patients on their way for transplant surgery. Many states have only one designated transplantation hospital, and patients must arrive at the transplant center within a few short hours of receiving the call that a matching organ is available. Angel Flight has pilots on standby who can get the patient to the transplant center in time for the life-saving surgery.

To find out more, or to make a donation, go to: angelflightsoars.org/patient-services/patient-services-transports-for-transplants.

BECOME AN AMBASSADOR. Reach out to your state's organ transplant organization to see how you can help.

unos.org
organdonationalliance.org

INTERACT WITH TODD AND SHARE YOUR IDEAS. You can contact Todd through his blog at: mymiracleman.com or you can email him at **mymiraclemantoddhensel@gmail.com.**

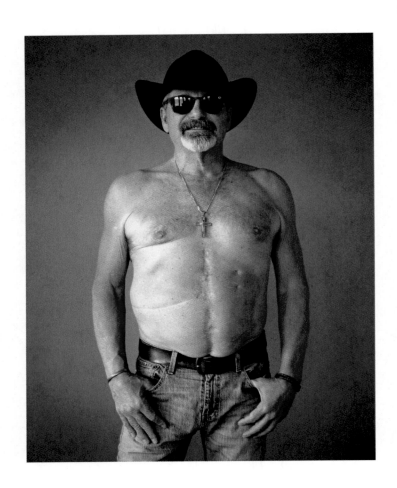

AFTERWORD

~

INFINITE GRATITUDE TO DR. VIANNA, FOR LISTENING TO HIS HEART, WALKING INTO TODD'S HOSPITAL ROOM IN DETROIT, FIGHTING THE POWERS THAT BE FOR THE OPPORTUNITY TO PERFORM THE MULTI-VISCERAL SURGERY ON TODD IN INDIANA, AND ULTIMATELY CHRISTENING TODD HIS "MIRACLE MAN."

Thank you for all the good you do every day to save lives.

To the angel bush pilot, with a request to please come forward if you happen to read this book—we would so love to thank you.

To Dr. Burcin Ekser at Indiana University, for taking the time to speak with us and providing his unique, invaluable insight on developments in the world of organ transplants in the past 15 years.

To Dean Graves, whose gift of artistic and technical expertise were invaluable to the completion of this book.

To Mary Bryant, our amazing editor and now friend, for jumping into this project with all her heart, soul and brilliance.

To Josh, Jarod, and Jacklyn, for being Todd's reasons for choosing to fight to live. To my children, Leah and Louis, for being my eternal, profound source of inspiration and love.

To Sandra, for recognizing me this time around and allowing me to assist in your journey of spreading healing through connecting with departed loved ones. To Cherlyn, for lifelong love and friendship, and for being the bridge for our reconnection. To Donna, my partner in crime, for insightful input (and bringing me tea or wine, depending on the time of day), and to her sister Marcie, for providing me a peaceful sanctuary in Hawaii to do much of the writing for this story.

And to my Todd, for the most beautiful, deep, and expansive love and passion you bring to our amazing life together, every single moment of every day.

Dr. Rodrigo Vianna, Carrie, and Todd
January 15, 2023, Miami Transplant Institute, Florida

Made in United States
Orlando, FL
26 July 2024